IMAGES OF ENGLAND

Hertford

Greetings from Hertford. This charming turn-of-the-twentieth-century postcard highlights the newly rebuilt All Saints church, a view of Port Hill, and Fore Street looking towards Shire Hall.

IMAGES OF ENGLAND

Hertford

Mervyn Miller

NONSUCH

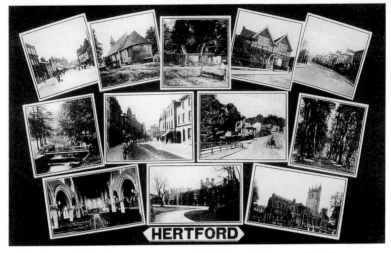

'Postage stamp' views of Hertford in 1904 include St Leonard Bengeo and the library,
Old Cross (second and fourth from left, top row); Castle Bridges (left, second row) and
Panshanger House (centre, bottom row).

First published 1996
This new pocket edition 2006
Images unchanged from first edition

Nonsuch Publishing Limited
The Mill, Brimscombe Port,
Stroud, Gloucestershire, GL5 2QG
www.nonsuch-publishing.com

Nosuch Publishing in an imprint of Tempus Publishing

British Library Cataloguing in Publication Data.v
A catalogue record for this book is available from the British Library.

ISBN 1-84588-279-2

Typesetting and origination by Nonsuch Publishing Limited
Printed in Great Britain by Oaklands Book Services Limited

Contents

Acknowledgements

In selecting the illustrations for this book, I have tried to avoid those used in recent publications about Hertford. The vast majority have been drawn from the collections of the Hertford Museum. I should like to thank Andrea George, Curator, together with Margaret Harris and Rosemary Bennett for their help: it was a privilege to be allowed free access to the comprehensive collection of historic postcards and photographs, and a pleasurable and daunting task to make the final choice. Thanks are also due to the following for their permission to reproduce the illustrations itemised below:

Christine Shearman of the Hertfordshire Local Studies Collection, pages 13 (upper), 27 (lower), 31 (upper), 32 (upper), 35 (upper), 41 (upper), 56 (upper), 60 (upper), 74 (upper), 90 (upper), 92 (lower), 96 (upper), 97 (upper and lower), 98 (upper), 106 (upper and lower), 108 (lower), 116, 123 (lower), 124 (lower); Kate Thompson, County Archivist, page 119 (upper and lower); McMullen and Sons Limited page 54 (lower), page 81 (upper and lower), page 82 (upper and lower); Hertford Society, page 129 (lower); James Barber, page 31 (lower), page 73. Finally, Sheila Murray transcribed the text and captions from my usual chaotic notes.

Introduction

Hertford's location determined its historic role. A marshy plain crossed by three winding streams – the Rivers Lea, Mimram and Beane, which joined together, and flowed eastwards towards the site of Ware, gathering the River Rib in the process, afforded a crossing for the main route northwards from London in Saxon times. The first Synod of the English Church was convened on the site in 673, and the Lea later formed the boundary between Saxon Wessex and the Danelaw. Saxon villages had been established at Bengeo and Hertingfordbury, and two fortified burghs, north and south of the Lea crossing, the present Millbridge, were founded by Edward the Elder in 911 and 912. To the west, overlooking the crossing, a motte and bailey castle was reconstructed by the Normans shortly after 1066, and the town mill adjacent was recorded in the Domesday survey of 1087. The Castle precinct, which belonged to the Crown until 1630, is defined by enclosing flint curtain walls of the late twelfth century, with an impressive double moat, traces of which can be seen in the hollowed land between the postern gate and Castle Street, and the line continues eastwards through Parliament Square and along The Wash, reflecting the dominance of the Castle and its influence on the borough's development. The Castle Gatehouse was rebuilt in brick in 1460-5 by order of Edward IV, and is the only major survival of the extensive structures, which included 'The King's Great Hall' within the bailey. The Scottish Kings David II and James I, and the French King John, were imprisoned in the castle: in the Tudor era Elizabeth I spent much of her childhood there, and Mary Queen of Scots was confined there before being taken northwards to Tutbury. The Salisburys of Hatfield were granted the freehold in 1630, and still hold the title: their relative the Marquess of Downshire remodelled the Gatehouse in the 1790s. In 1911 the Castle was leased to Hertford Borough Council, and transferred to East Herts District Council upon local government reorganisation in 1974. Appropriately Hertford Town Council took a major tenancy. In 1996 the major part of the grounds were in process of transfer to East Herts DC, under a gift from Lord Salisbury.

The town developed through the centuries, with twin churches, and market places – in Old Cross and behind Maidenhead Street, but these were replaced by St Andrews and All Saints, which were both rebuilt in the late nineteenth century. In 1888, clearance at Old Cross for the new library building brought fragments of old St Mary's to light, which were assembled into a drinking fountain. St Andrew Street and Cowbridge became thronged with buildings and clogged with horse-drawn traffic making its way over the toll-financed Millbridge – charges were finally abolished on Boxing Day 1893. The 'south burgh' emerged as the main commercial centre, with shops and inns along Fore Street and Railway Street/ Maidenhead Street. Many imposing buildings bear witness to the town's importance in the seventeenth and eighteenth centuries but rivalry with Ware, a few miles east, was intense. Hertford emerged as a prosperous local centre, with industries based on milling and malting. The rivers and watercourses, with their marshy meadows, helped to preserve green wedges penetrating the town centre, with higher land, particularly the wooded bluff of Bengeo, defining the setting. The rivers were important for transport and milling. The Lea Navigation provided a ready connection with London markets, and was improved to Ware in 1739, and Hertford in 1769. The New Cut, with its lock on King's Meads, isolated Folly Island, which was developed with small houses in the nineteenth century. Six mills were recorded in Domesday, and the last to remain operational, Sele Roller Mill, closed in 1988 and has been converted to housing. The same fate has overtaken several maltings, but the complex at Old Cross Wharf, though no longer operational, survives virtually intact. Peter McMullen began brewing in 1827, and the firm's brewery in Hartham Lane was opened in 1891.

A modern local authority, with administrative responsibilities, began to emerge in the mid-nineteenth century. Already, the construction of the new Shire Hall, designed by James Adams in 1771, showed the town's importance for corn trading, courts-of-law, and social events. Jane Austen is supposed to have based Meryton in Pride and Prejudice on Hertford, and Elizabeth Bennet, whose family home was Epcombs, Hertingfordbury, would have met Mr Darcy in Shire Hall's handsome Assembly Room (beautifully restored in 1988-90). For local education, the Richard Hale School was opened, near All Saints churchyard, in 1619 while the Bluecoat Boys School came to Hertford in 1666, followed by the opening of the Girl's School in 1788 which was rebuilt in 1906 and closed in 1984. The Eastern Counties Railway reached Hertford in 1843 but its station, Hertford East since 1923, was rebuilt in a florid Jacobean style in 1888. The Great Northern Railway opened a branch from Welwyn to Cowbridge in 1858 which closed in 1924 and was more recently demolished. It was replaced with a new station, Hertford North, high above North Road on the Stevenage line, which opened in 1924. The town expanded east along Ware Road, south along Queens Road, and westwards towards Hertingfordbury. The surrounding countryside still retained its unspoilt quality in the stewardship of the great estates at Balls Park (built 1637), Panshanger (built 1806: demolished 1953-4) and Goldings (rebuilt 1874).

Hertfordshire County Council was established, by Act of Parliament, in 1889, but for many years, due to poor east-west communication, the Council met in London. In 1934 the Leahoe estate bordering Peg's Lane was purchased, and in 1939, County Hall, a competition-winning design by James and Bywaters, with Rowland Pierce, was completed, just as war broke out. After 1945, Hertford, like many small towns, expanded and was replanned to remove through traffic from its narrow, mediaeval streets. The relief road, Gascoyne Way, destroyed the town's relationship with All Saints church, cut cruelly through Castle Street, cut off the water meadows to the west, and destroyed the historic turning at the end of St Andrew Street. Yet it enabled the preservation of much of the centre as a Conservation Area. Through the vigilance of the Civic Society, central area redevelopment around Bircherley Green was toned down, although its pastiche buildings fail to match the quality of the historic streets nearby. Hertford Borough passed into the expanded East Hertfordshire District Council area in April 1974, but its traditions are maintained by the Hertford Town Council. East Herts has taken its conservation duties seriously, and recently promoted the resurvey, in liaison with English Heritage, of the historic buildings list for the town. In September 1996 the new list with over 350 protected buildings was launched, complementing the Council's repaving of the town centre, and its efforts to remove traffic from the historic core.

Dr Mervyn Miller
September 1996

One

A Bustling Borough

In 1904, The Wash was a busy shopping street. While the buildings on the right remain today, everything left of the three storey building, then McMullen's offices, has been redeveloped including the town mill – the miller's house is centre left.

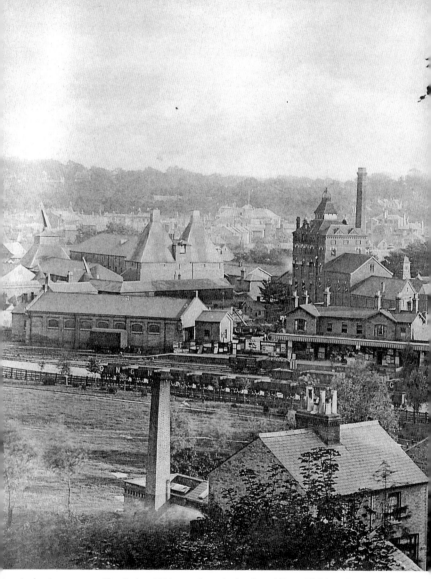

A pleasing prospect, Hertford, c. 1904, seen from the heights of 'Bryn Allt' (now known as 'Whitacre'), Port Hill. In the middle distance, beyond Hartham is the Great Northern

Cowbridge station, with McMullen's Brewery rising behind, and to the right, the Hope Brewery which they took over.

Fore Street was frequented by the 'carriage trade' in the 1890s: the top-hated driver waits outside Neale's, with its awnings shading the pavement. In the middle distance is the handsome pedimented Corn Exchange, opened in 1859.

The sweep of Fore Street in 1904, looking towards Shire Hall, with its clock by John Briant, installed in 1824.

Shire Hall, designed by James Adam, was completed in 1771, but altered in 1885 and 1902. The Assizes and Quarter Sessions were held there until 1971. This unusual view was taken in the mid 1950s, when Neale's old premises were redeveloped, revealing virtually the whole façade.

Neale's furniture shop occupied the handsome mid-seventeenth century block on the corner of Fore Street and Market Place: the elaborate modelled 'pargetting' has been restored several times and survives but many of the Georgian shopfronts have disappeared.

Left: Two imposing neighbours in Fore Street. Gilbertson and Page proudly displayed their Royal Arms for supplying game food and dog biscuits. The building, with its Egyptian style façade survives intact to this day, after many changes of use. Taylor's ironmongers, centre, is now the Midland Bank.

Below: The post office, with its ornate orange brick and dressed limestone frontage, was designed by H. Johnson and built by H. Norris in 1890. It occupied the site of the Chequer Inn and its crowded tenements behind in the yard.

Opposite above: The timber-framed structure of the Salisbury Arms, in Fore Street, dates from the fifteenth century, although its exterior has been renovated many times since. It originally had an open yard with galleries behind. This view dates from 1902.

Opposite below: The former Dimsdale Arms fronted Fore Street: it is now a Hertfordshire University residence. Known as the Duncombe Arms, it achieved notoriety in the 1832 election, one of the most corrupt of the period. It was renamed after Thomas Dimsdale, the physician who innoculated Catherine the Great against smallpox.

DIMSDALE HOTEL, HERTFORD, HERTS.

One of the Oldest and best appointed Hotels in the County.   Moderate Tariff.
Modern Carriages of all descriptions Let on Hire.   J. L. CAMPLING, *Proprietor.*

Also,

HUGMANS' LIVERY YARD,
College Mews, Hertford Heath, HERTFORD.

By Appointment to Haileybury College.   Carriages to Order.
Broxbourne Station, G.E., and Hertford, G.N.R.

In the mid 1890s Rayment's Grocers occupied the fine building in Fore Street which is now Barclay's Bank. The shopfront, with its distinctive Ionic columns was lost when Rayment's moved across the road: flyposters indicate the forthcoming change of address.

The narrow gap between Shire Hall and the Salisbury Arms constricted traffic for many years. Happily, the present view is virtually unchanged from this 1904 postcard, while traffic management has removed the congestion that threatened the town before Gascoyne Way was built in the 1960s.

Originally held in the Market Place outside Shire Hall, the open-air market moved to the gap alongside The Corn Exchange when the covered market behind it was built in 1889. This view with its characteristic hustle and bustle dates from the early 1930s.

18

This range of timber-framed buildings, with an overhanging 'jettied' front and solid brick chimneystack stood at the corner of Fore Street and South Street: it was swept away in the mid 1890s.

Shephard's, the plumbers and decorators (right), moved into the imposing corner block with its turret corner, when rebuilding took place.

In 1890 Wigginton's, Wine and Spirit Merchants, moved into this building which stood at the corner of Fore Street and Castle Street – their main premises were at the corner of St Andrew Street and Old Cross, where the name is still in use.

By 1920, the building was occupied by Bruton's, tailors, and the block was about to be cleared to create the space for Parliament Square and the War Memorial. This view was taken from the balcony of the Hertfordshire Mercury opposite.

The War Memorial, designed by Sir Aston Webb, was unveiled in 1921 – it was built of Portland stone from the same quarry as The Cenotaph in Whitehall. The hart was modelled by the sculptor Alfred Drury. Here the memorial's workmen put finishing touches to the surround, before the final demolition of the old buildings has been completed.

Demolition of Nightingale's shop is almost complete. Parliament Row took its name from terraced cottages in which Parliament met during sixteenth-century outbreaks of plague in London.

The battlemented lodge and gateway to the Castle Grounds were built around 1800 by the Marquess of Downshire. Occupied for many years by Longmore's the solicitors, the gateway was infilled in 1904, shortly after this postcard was published. At the left, Nos 21 and 23 Castle Street is a much altered fifteenth-century open-hall house.

Pimlico Hill lay at the skewed junction of Castle Street and West Street. It was swept away by the construction of Gascoyne Way in 1964. The Chaseside Motor Co. displays the 1938 Ford Prefect and Pilot in its showrooms: today its successor, Trimoco, occupies rebuilt premises to the west.

Seen here in 1890, No. 27 West Street dated from the seventeenth century and was altered and extended around 1800, when it was the home of William Archer, a miller and manufacturer of linseed oil. In the 1950s-1970s, Gordon Moodey, the historian and enthusiast for Hertfordshire's historic buildings lived here.

Bridgeman House, named after Charles Bridgeman, organist of All Saints church from 1791 to 1872, was built in 1649. This rear view was taken around 1880, before the wing at the left, used as a school, was rebuilt in brick.

Graveson and Robinson began business in Market Place. Around 1895 they acquired the property behind, fronting Salisbury Square and Maidenhead Street. This view was taken just prior to rebuilding with the familiar building which turns the corner, and has large display windows between cast-iron columns.

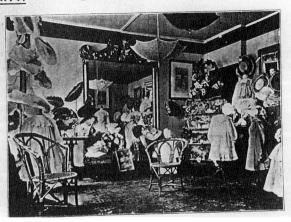

Graveson's boasted a wide selection of accessories for ladies of fashion in the 1890's, including broad-brimmed 'Gainsborough' hats and parasols.

Maidenhead Street lay behind Fore Street (and was known as 'Back Street' for many years). Its shops were more bustling and commercial. This 1910 view shows the rebuilt Green Dragon Hotel, above Spencer's Corner, at the right, with Pratt's, turning the corner to The Wash, on the left.

On 6 May 1917, fire destroyed an important part of the north frontage of Maidenhead Street: here the police and bystanders view the smouldering ruins.

Bull Plain was named after The Bull Inn, a much-altered fifteenth-century building, now occupied by Hertford Cameras. This view, in which it looks virtually derelict, dates from 1907.

On the west of Bull Plain lay a handsome seventeenth-century building, with a central courtyard and projecting wings. Badly damaged in the Zeppelin raid of 1915, it was demolished and rebuilt after the First World War. At the extreme right is Lombard House.

'Queen Anne Front' – Lombard House, of fifteenth century origin, was the home of Sir Henry Chauncy, barrister and author of *The Historical Antiquities of Hertfordshire* (1700). The handsome brick front was built in the mid-eighteenth century. The building is now occupied by the Hertford Club.

'Mary Ann Back'. The mediaeval origins of Lombard House are readily apparent in this 1927 view of its gables overhanging the River Lea, near Folly Bridge.

At its eastern end Fore Street led into Ware Road, while London Road branched off southwards (to the right). The Plough Inn stood at the junction, and is seen here in 1932, not long before it was rebuilt for road widening. An office block now marks its site.

London Road, Hertford.

40.

A few hundred yards down London Road stood the Cowper Testimonial School, opened in this fine Tudor-style building in 1841. It closed in 1957, and was later demolished when the re-aligned dual carriageway, London Road, was driven through the site to meet Gascoyne Way.

Two

North of Mill Bridge

Old Cross formed the hub of the 'North Borough', and became a traffic black spot. Here, at the turn of the century, a hay wagon and a governess cart pass leisurely in front of the newly built library.

Mill Bridge, and the river crossing led to Old Cross, flanked by the town mill, and a row of shops which was demolished in 1927, except for McMullen's at the extreme right. Wiggintons can be seen ahead in the far distance in this 1904 view.

The Woolpack stood on the corner of Old Cross and Mill Bridge until 1927, when it was demolished, and the road was widened to cross the river on a new bridge. This photograph was taken shortly before the demolition: the new Woolpack now stands next to the rebuilt bridge.

Floods at Mill Bridge, photographed by Arthur Elsden in 1880. Wickham's Brewery, a complex clutter of timber-clad buildings is at the left, with a portion of the town mill (Ilott's) on the right.

Old Cross Wharf overlooks the Upper Winding Basin. Although damaged in 1944, the site contains one of the oldest maltings in Hertford, with traces of sixteenth-century brickwork. The conical kiln roof and cowl, seen in this turn-of-the-century view, remain one of the landmarks of the riverside.

The Folly Island was formed when the Lea cut was made. The old water works, photographed by Elsden in the 1880s, took water from the river and pumped it across Hartham and up to the reservoir in Bengeo.

River Lea, Hertford

The Barge Inn dates from the mid-nineteenth century and the terraced housing was constructed between 1863 and 1896 by the Andrews brothers, whose middle names are commemorated in Frampton Street and Thornton Street. Lombard House is on the right and beyond the warehouses, behind which lay Bircherley Green.

Above: Building sites have provided spectator fascination since time immemorial. At Old Cross, in 1888, the old cottages were demolished, and the cellars filled in, for the new library. In the background the site of Beckwith's original antique showrooms can be seen.

Right: The library (which also housed an Art School) was designed by (Sir) Reginald Blomfield in 1888. It was opened by A. J. Balfour, who had been the Divisional MP, and later became Prime Minister.

Above: During excavations of the library site in 1888, the remains of the thirteenth-century church of St Mary the Less were discovered. They were photographed for W. F. Andrews, whose amateur enthusiasm for archaeology led to the founding of Hertford Museum in 1914.

Left: Out of the jigsaw of stone fragments seen above, this drinking fountain, with a lancet opening above, was built in 1890 alongside the library. The remaining stones are still stored in the basement of the museum on Bull Plain.

Opposite above: Cowbridge leads from Old Cross towards Port Vale. Halfway along lay The Traveller's Rest, seen here in a pre-1862 Elsden photograph. The bakery next door was replaced by the Cowbridge Halls in 1891-1, and beyond that the United Reform church was built in 1862-3.

Below: The north side of Cowbridge was rebuilt during the later nineteenth century. The houses at the right replaced Cowbridge House, largely demolished after Cowbridge station opened in 1858. In the distance is the Hertford Baptist church, 1905-6, which appears newly-built in this view.

St Andrew Street contains some of the most imposing buildings in Hertford. At the right is Wiggintons, refaced in the early eighteenth century, and other Queen Anne buildings, contrasting with the mediaeval gables and plasterwork across the road in this 1870s Elsden photograph.

In this early 1920s view of St Andrew Street a group of boys pose in front of a seventeenth century double-gabled house, ornamental with nineteenth-century 'Gothick' barge boards.

At the turn of the twentieth century, Hertford Hygienic Laudry occupied this fine mediaeval building at the west end of St Andrew Street near the junction with North Road and Hertingfordbury Road. The building was demolished in 1964 for the road realignment in connection with the construction of Gascoyne Way.

St. Andrew's Street and Chapel, Hertford

The Ebenezer Baptist chapel stood on the fork of the road oppoiste the laundry. All the buildings seen in this 1904 picture were demolished in 1964, with the exception of the cottage with dormer at the extreme right. The chapel was rebuilt, setback from the road on the site of the demolished Cold Bath Inn.

'Eighteenth-century brickwork of the choicest sort' was the comment of historian Gordon Moodey, when writing about Yeomanry House, built about 1725, and one of the grandest residences in Hertford. Happily it still appears virtually as seen in this fine turn-of-the-century photograph.

Photographed in about 1891 by Elsden, the Old Verger's House looks as if it will not last out the nineteenth century. Two years later it was restored as St Nicholas Hall, with a large extension replacing derelict cottages behind: the building is now occupied by Beckwith's Antiques, who moved from Old Cross.

This postcard shows St Nicholas Hall in 1905, and the skilful restoration of its fifteenth-century timber-framed frontage, one of the finest mediaeval buildings in Hertford.

Looking east along St Andrew Street in 1904, the familiar juxtaposition of Cawthorne House with the spire of the rebuilt St Andrew's church looming above dominates the scene. The buildings at the extreme left and right disappeared in 1964, however.

North Road looks like a winter wonderland under heavy snowfall in this 1890s Elsden photograph. Their studio was in the building at the right, now part of Waters' Garage, from 1859 to 1872. Beyond are the gable ends of the Cold Bath Inn and the Hertford Laundry, below St Andrew's spire.

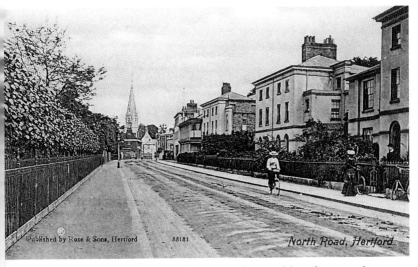

Published by Rose & Sons, Hertford   85181   *North Road, Hertford*

From a viewpoint further west along North Road, the elegance of the early nineteenth-century North Crescent can be seen, in 1904, complete with front railings, and without some of the insensitive alterations which have since marred its style. The architect was Thomas Smith who lived at North Road House opposite.

Then known as The Infirmary, the County Hospital had extensive well-kept gardens in 1904. It was designed by Thomas Smith and built in 1832-3, with assistance from Henry Cowper of Tewin Water. Its future is now insecure.

Drs Burnett-Smith, Odell and Evans, at left; and Shelly, Boyd and Dunn at right with the nursing staff of the County Hospital, which took its new name in 1908. Miss Studderd, the Matron and her staff look the epitome of starched propriety.

Three

Castle and Celebration

The Ceremony of the Keys. The Marquess of Salisbury conveyed a lease of the Castle to Hertford Borough Council in July 1912. Osmond Henry McMullen, Mayor of Hertford, paid for the new gateway to The Wash, which was opened with due ceremony.

The fifteenth-century brick-built gate house is the major surviving building of Hertford Castle. It was turned into a residence by the Marquess of Downshire in the 1790s when the south wing (right) was built and the 'Gothick' windows were installed. This fine late nineteenth-century view is taken from the Castle Bridges over the River Lea.

Hertford Castle.

After 1912 the grounds of the Castle became a public pleasure garden, with a much-frequented tennis lawn. In 1937 a two-bay north wing was added, at the right of the ivy-clad gatehouse.

The Old Wall, Hertford Castle.

26.

The twelfth-century curtain wall has been restored since 1912 and the ivy cut back. The greenhouse at the end of the broadwalk has long since disappeared.

The Old Gate, Hertford Castle.

The postern now gives access through the hollow, which marked the double moat, to Castle Street. In this pre-1914 view there is a tangible atmosphere of romantic decay.

Hertford celebrated its millenium with an elaborate historical pageant staged in the Castle grounds June 19-July 4 1914. The first tableau showed the meeting of the first Synod of the English Church AD 673.

The second tableau showed the defeat of the Danes by Alfred the Great in AD 896.

The dramatic siege and capture of Hertford Castle by the forces of the French Dauphin in December 1216 was enacted in the third tableau.

After a turbulent period, with royal prisoners including King David II of Scotland and King John of France, the wife of King Henry VI of England, Margaret of Anjou, granted a charter to the Borough in 1451 to hold a horse-fair in the town.

Mayor, Frank Page, and Corporation, 1912. To the right is Dr J. Burnett-Smith, and to the left, Alfred Baker, Town Clerk. Lieut-Colonel Page was killed in action in France in 1918.

The Wigginton boys, centre, and friends, enact the Children's Corporation in 1895.

A. J. Balfour (1848-1930), Divisional MP for Hertford in the late nineteenth century: Prime Minister 1902-5. In June 1914 he returned to Hertford, seen here accompanied by the Mayor, W. F. Andrews, in the Castle grounds.

The Honor of Hertford. On 1 October 1925, the Marquess of Salisbury presided at a ceremony where a 'Standard of Honor' was presented to the Mayor, Josiah Wren, by the York Herald. Schoolchildren packed the Castle grounds, and newsreel cameras recorded the event.

In this late nineteenth-century Elsden photograph Fore Street, in front of the Corn Exchange, is crowded, with a band present. It may have been taken in 1897, Queen Victoria's Diamond Jubilee year, when Sir George Faudel Phillips of Balls Park, then Lord Mayor of London, received the Freedom of Hertford Borough.

The Golden Jubilee of 1887 was marked by a dinner for the elderly, held in the Corn Exchange.

A similar event was held in 1902 to mark the Coronation of King Edward VII and Queen Alexandra.

In 1911, the Drill Hall at Port Hill hosted the Coronation Dinner for King George V and Queen Mary.

The King had visited Hertford on July 23 1906, when he was still the Prince of Wales, to open the new dormitories and chapel at Christ's Hospital Girls School. He arrived at Cowbridge station, where the approach road was decorated with a garlanded arch, with one shilling seats on the site of Ekins Builders works, at left.

Before joining the carriage procession through the town, the Prince inspected a guard of honour in the station yard.

On May 12 1937 King George VI and Queen Elizabeth were crowned at Westminister Abbey. Hertford held its own Coronation procession, with elaborately decorated tradesmen's vans passing over Millbridge.

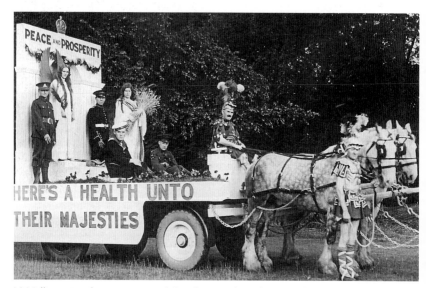

McMullens rejected motor power, and their float was drawn by two of their immaculate dray-horses. Regrettably 'peace and prosperity' was to be shattered two years later in September 1939.

Four

Churches

The Methodist chapel presented a Gothic front between Regency and early Victorian houses. Seen here in 1920, the chapel was rebuilt in the 1960s, but its hall, partly obscured by the tree to the left, survives.

The twelfth-century church of St Leonard at Bengeo was in poor condition in the late nineteenth century, with an ugly gabled roof over its curved apsidal east end.

The interior likewise had a derelict and unkempt appearance. The church was replaced for regular worship by Holy Trinity, in New Road, built in 1855. Happily it was restored, and is recognised as a fine example of Norman architecture.

Church Street, seen in 1904, led from Fore Street to the densely tree-lined churchyard of All Saints, a green 'lung' south of the congested town centre. All changed in 1964, when Gascoyne Way was cut through, separating the church from the town.

The principal church in the town, All Saints had been altered over the years, but still reflected its mediaeval origins. Its organist Charles Bridgeman (1778-1873) served from the age of 13 until his death – a remarkable record.

All Saints was gutted by fire on 21 December 1891 – the external shell stood starkly in the grey winter light.

The interior was open to the elements – a chaotic mess of charred timber and collapsed rubble. The Corn Exchange was used as a temporary church for three years.

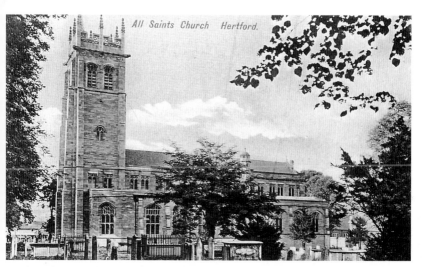

The replacement church was designed by Paley, Austin and Paley of Lancaster, and built of Runcorn sandstone. The new church cost £12,500 and was dedicated by the Bishop of St Albans on 20 February 1895. The Victoria Tower, costing a further £12,000 was completed a decade later.

The bells were destroyed in the fire, and a new peal was cast. The Church Council were photographed by Elsden shortly before the new bells were hung.

St. Andrew's Church, Hertford

55179

Above: The Friends Meeting House in Railway Street was built in 1669-70 at a cost of £293 12s, and is said to be the oldest in continuous use. Its plain exterior is virtually unchanged.

Right: George Fox, founder of the Quakers, visited Hertford three times and his chair stands in the entrance hall beneath the gallery.

Opposite above: St Andrew's church was apparently in a parlous state and was rebuilt 1869-70. This rare Elsden photograph shows the old church in the early 1860s.

Opposite below: Designed by J. Johnson, the new St Andrew's was built alongside the old tower in nine months by Dove Bros of London. In Gothic Revival style, the new church was completed in 1875-6 by the construction of a new tower and spire funded by Earl Cowper and Abel Smith.

Left: Christ church, Port Vale was built in 1868 to serve an area which was rapidly developing. Built in the Gothic Revival style, it was paid for by Abel Smith of Woodhall Park. Demolished in the 1960s, houses now occupy its site.

Below: The Roman Catholic church of the Immaculate Conception and St Joseph was built in 1859-61, and designed by Henry Clutton, in a thirteenth century Gothic style with French influence. Appropriately its site adjoined that of St Mary's Priory, destroyed by Henry VIII.

Five

Outskirts and Rural Surroundings

Hertford began to expand outwards in the mid-nineteenth century. This 1905 postcard of Ware Road shows newly-built suburban houses, with a distant view of the imposing Union Workhouse, later a school and eventually demolished in the 1960s for the new police station.

The rivers of Hertford, with their water meadows, give the town a most attractive setting. Watersmeet marks the confluence of the Lea and Rib near Bengeo, and has changed little since 1905.

Hartham and the water meadow of the River Beane is one of the town's major recreation areas, seen from Port Hill.

The New River was constructed between 1608 and 1613 to provide fresh water for London from the Chadwell Spring between Hertford and Ware. The circular Chadwell Basin was later supplemented by water drawn from a gauge on the River Lea.

This Elsden photograph of 1889 shows the Chadwell Basin without water, presumably for cleaning. In the foreground is one of the eighteenth-century marker stones: beyond can be seen the Great Eastern railway line from Ware to Hertford.

HERTFORD.—THE LOCK, RIVER LEA

Hertford lock controlled the water levels in the Lea Navigation downstream from the mill race to Dicker Mill. John Smeaton and Thomas Telford were among the engineers who improved the Lea waterways. As late as the First World War, improvements were made to enable 100-ton ships to reach Hertford.

The water meadows of the Beane, looking towards Molewood Road in 1904. Development climbs Port Hill towards Bengeo, where the distant water tower can be seen. At the right is the Great Northern line from Cowbridge to Welwyn. Beane Road was later built across the meadows, and the new GNR line to Stevenage was opened in 1920.

Balls Park was the most important country house on the southern fringe of Hertford. It was approached from London Road through this gateway, guarded by a nineteenth-century lodge. These survive but the main road was diverted in the 1960s.

One of the outstanding mid seventeenth century mansions, Balls Park was later the home of the agricultural reformer Viscount 'turnip' Townshend. In the late nineteenth century, Sir George Faudel Phillips bought the property: he served as Lord Mayor of London in 1897. In 1946 the house became a teacher training college; it now belongs to the University of Hertford.

Queen's Road was developed from the mid-nineteenth century, west of All Saints churchyard. High on the hill stood Elmsfield, a large Victorian house which faced Hagsdell Road, and its lodge can be seen at the left in this 1904 view.

Looking northwards towards Hertford town centre, Queens Road had an impressive sweep, despite the stark outlines of the pruned and pollarded trees. To the right the newly completed tower of All Saints can be seen.

Port Hill leads from the junction with Cowbridge upwards to Bengeo. Apart from the lack of traffic, the view has changed little since this 1904 postcard was issued. The foreground railings mark the embankment of the bridge over the Cowbridge-Welwyn line. In the far distance the lodge to Warren Woods can be seen.

Bengeo Road (now Bengeo Street) had a quiet rural charm at the turn of the century. In the middle distance on the right is the Globe Inn, further along on the left stood the Greyhound, which provided ample pause for refreshment on the way to, or from, Wadesmill.

New Road leads past Holy Trinity church, then turns towards Bengeo Hall, and runs on to Ware Park. At the turn of the century these houses stood in isolation. Regrettably the magnificent trees were felled, as the road was widened and housing was developed before and after the Second World War.

Beating the Bounds of Bengeo Parish: Alfred Graveson; Alfred Baker, Town Clerk; Tanner, Rate Collector; H. G. Andrews and O. G. Rose, mid 1920s.

The terraces and semi-detached houses in Hertingfordbury Road were built in the early twentieth century on the Nursery behind the County Hospital. A total lack of traffic has tempted the girl with the perambulator to pose on the unmetalled road: today a dual carriageway extension of Gascoyne Way hastens traffic towards Hatfield.

Hertingfordbury village itself was remote in 1904. The familiar sign of the White Horse Inn can be seen in the distance. Hertingfordbury regained its repose in the 1970s when a bypass was built: behind its sixteenth-century frontage the White Horse has expanded as a modern hotel.

A solitary car halts outside Dell Cottage on Hertingfordbury Road. Beyond, at the left, can be seen one of the lodges to Panshanger. Today both properties have been cut off from the new main road, and separated by the roundabout at the start of the Hertingfordbury bypass.

THE LAKE, PANSHANGER.

Panshanger, overlooking the Mimram Valley, was built by the Cowpers in 1806, in a position left for it in Humphrey Repton's landscaping. The rambling Gothic style house was demolished in 1953-4 after the death of Lady Desborough. This tranquil view dates from 1904.

Six

At Work

Barge loading at Old Cross Wharf, *c.* 1900. Water transport of bulk loads to the heart of Hertford was common until the Second World War.

The mills and manufactories of Hertford made extensive use of its abundant water for power and processing. Horns Mill lay on the Brickendon Road, and drew its water from the Lea. This Elsden photograph dates from 1858 when the mill was rebuilt and the mill race redug.

Horns Mill specialised in linseed oil production in the mid-nineteenth century. In 1890 it was sold to William Webb who began production of chamois leather, and installed fulling stocks. This postcard dates from the turn of the twentieth century.

Leather drying on open-air racks in the 1930s – a striking photograph by Norman L. Hare.

Joan Newman making gloves at Webb & Co. in the 1950s. Production ceased in the late 1960s, and Horns Mill was demolished in 1973 – houses now stand on its site.

Right: Toothbrush manufacture at Addis's in 1976. By this time plastic and nylon had replaced bone and natural bristle. The firm also diversified into plastic household ware, still made at their factories in Wales.

Below: Addis began to manufacture toothbrushes in 1780, but only came to Hertford after the First World War, taking over the buildings of the Hertford Steam Laundry. This smart streamlined building was designed by Donald Hamilton in 1935. Addis's Hertford factory closed in 1993.

Parlophone, a branch of Columbia, opened a gramophone record factory in Hertford in 1928. This photograph shows the manager, Mr J. L. Tubbert, with test pressings. The works was built near to the power station off Mead Lane.

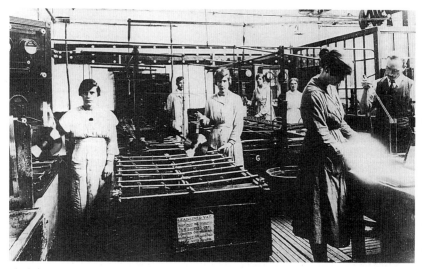

The ladies are working at the vats where the wax masters were electrotyped in copper sulphate to form the stampers from which the records were pressed in shellac-brittle, breakable 78 rpm discs. Parlophone was taken over by EMI in 1931, and production at Hertford ceased in 1938.

Dicker Mill was rebuilt, and moved from its position near the Priory when the Lea Navigation cut was made. It produced linseed oil and cattle cake from the turn of the century, which were transported by barge, but ceased production in the 1920s.

Ewen and Tomlinson were one of the principal builders' merchants and sawmills in the town, located at the head of St John's Street on the historic site of Hertford Priory. On 25 August 1907 they suffered a severe fire: the nearby Roman Catholic church at the right of the picture seems to have escaped unharmed.

Mill Bridge in 1927, with Wickham's Brewery at right, and a row of shops fronting the Town Mill at left. Recorded in the Domesday Survey, it was run by the Ilotts from 1855. This complex of buildings was severely damaged by a flying bomb in July 1944.

Repaired, the mill lasted for a few more years after the war and entered a tranquil decline. Production ceased in the 1960s and the buildings were demolished. Castle Hall, built in 1973, now occupies the site.

The Hertford Brewery 1891

Above: McMullen's began brewing in 1827. They acquired a site on Millbridge, then expanded over the Hope Brewery in the process. McMullens built their new brewery in 1891, covering the wedge-shaped site, and the openwork cupola which crowns the main building is still a local landmark.

Right: McMullen's 'Old Fashioned Home Brewed' Ginger Beer won a Gold Medal at the Paris Exhibition in 1912, a success commemorated at a parade in Hertford.

Above: The staff of Sworder and Longmore pose for Elsden in the gateway of the Castle Lodge. This was infilled in 1904, and the practice has since expanded into the adjoining house.

Right: Philip Longmore, Town Clerk 1829-66, through the period which saw Hertford emerge as a modern borough – a fine Elsden portrait. Generations of Longmores served borough and county councils.

Opposite above: Captain Howes, Bottled Beer and Mineral Water Manager, second from left, poses with his staff outside the brewery in 1925.

Opposite below: Mr T. Wilson, Brewing Manager, surveying the fermenting wort, in the original copper-lined wooden vats in the brewery, 1972.

F. Walter Taylor, confectioner and muffin man, was a well-known local character in the early years of the century. He tried to retain the market rights at Old Cross by erecting a stall annually.

Seven

At School and At Play

Members of the League of Pity, following a performance of Cinderella given in the grounds of Bryn Allt, Port Hill, in 1893.

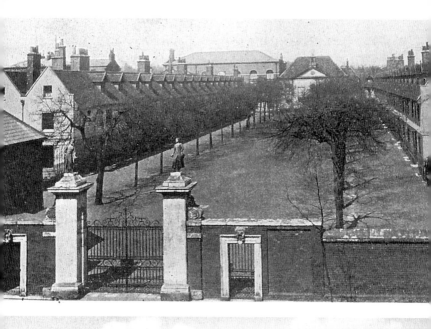

Right: Groups of boys, wearing their characteristic blue robes, are lined up in front of the Writing School, supervised by bowler-hatted procters. This photograph is pre-1900, when the building was refronted.

Below: A few years later, pinafore-clad girls march in pairs, forming a long crocodile progressing towards the Dining Hall, off to the left of the photograph.

Opposite above: Founded by King Edward VI in 1552, Christ's Hospital School moved to Hertford in 1666 after the Great Fire of London. Their new buildings were completed in 1695, and housed the younger boys in dormitory blocks facing each other across a tree-lined yard.

Opposite below: In 1788 the Christ's Hospital girls came to Hertford and were housed in Nos 121-129 Fore Street. In 1902 all the boys moved to Horsham, and the dormitories were rebuilt as eight large houses in 1904. The rebuilt school and its new chapel was opened by the Prince of Wales, later King George V. After the school closed in 1984, the dormitories were converted to offices.

A scene in the gas-lit Dining Hall, pre-1904. The large pipe organ (right) was used during assembly.

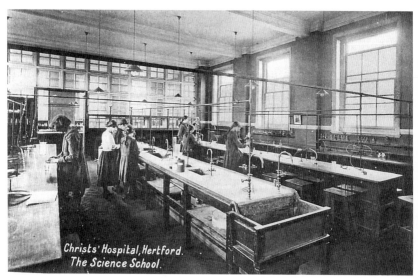

Christs' Hospital, Hertford.
The Science School.

Education for girls improved greatly at the turn of the century, and the new buildings included an up-to-date science laboratory.

Richard Hale founded the Grammar School which bore his name in 1617. It occupied premises east of All Saints churchyard, now on the edge of Gascoyne Way. The original seventeenth-century building, which had one large open classroom, survives in a much-altered form.

Brought under control of the County Council, the school was rebuilt in 1930 adjoining Peg's Lane: in this view it is ready to receive the first pupils. The original door of the old school was installed in a place of honour in the entrance hall. Greatly expanded, the Richard Hale School is now part of the county's comprehensive system.

The Faudel Phillips School was formed from All Saints Infants School and the School of Industry, which trained girls for domestic service. Here Class II are shown at long desks, girls and boys rigorously separated, with a stepped arrangement that enabled the teacher to keep an eye on everything.

By contrast, the refined young ladies, girls and infant boys at Miss Morris's private preparatory school on Ware Road, 1905, appear more relaxed.

All schools had their own sports teams: the Cowper Testimonial School Football Club of 1936-7 were ready to play all-comers.

Dressed in their best for the 1925 school outing, pupils of Port Vale School line up in front of their motor coach.

Built as a sumptious Tudor-style country house by Robert Smith in 1871-7, Goldings passed to Dr Barnados and became the William Baker Technical School in 1923. After closure in 1967, it was occupied by the County Surveyor's Department, but was offered for sale in 1996.

Above: Dr Barnado's taught rudimentary crafts to the orphans in its care: in this picture the bootmakers are hard at work.

Opposite above: The Hertford Improvement Society engaged in debate and discussion. In 1891, they are seen grouped around their President, T. J. Sworder, centre, in the garden of his home, Wallfields. This is now the East Hertfordshire District Council offices.

Below: Gilbert and Sullivan operettas have been staple fare for amateur musical groups for over a century. The cast of The Mikado pose for Elsden in February 1908.

A smart turn-out was the order of the day when Sworder and Longmore played cricket against fellow solicitors, Hawkins & Co. of Hitchin, on 20 July 1905, held on the cricket oval in Warren Park Road.

Left: The Good Companions raised money for charity: in 1946 their competition-winning darts team was presented with the silver cup by the Pearly King.

Opposite above: In August 1911, the smartly kitted-out Hertford Boy Scouts group made camp in the grounds of Panshanger House on the western outskirts of Hertford.

Below: In 1893, the Wigginton children and friends presented a patriotic pageant in their garden.

Spartan pleasures were provided by the outdoor swimming pool at Hartham, built over a branch of the Lea: water flowed through a filter at one end and out at the other – the bottom was mud. The bath enclosure is seen in 1934 shortly before it was replaced by a proper outdoor lido nearby.

Notwithstanding the primitive conditions, these boys, photographed by Elsden at the turn of the twentieth century, appear to be enjoying their bathing.

Winter sports – the boys of Bengeo College, a preparatory school which sent many pupils to Haileybury, have a fine time in the snow in the grounds of Daneshill, Warren Park Road.

Skaters waltz – with St Andrew's church as a backdrop, elegantly dressed skaters venture on to the frozen Castle Mead, photographed by Elsden in the severe winter of 1881-2.

The Whit Monday fete on Hartham included obstacles for the active, as shown by this Elsden photograph from the turn of the century.

Others have always enjoyed quieter leisure pursuits. This fine photograph, 'At the local' was taken by Norman L. Hare in the 1930s – unfortunately he did not identify the venue.

The Castle Cinema, in The Wash, opened in August 1914. The bench seats in the front stalls packed in patrons, and the pit screened the orchestra, disbanded after the first talkie presentation, King of the Khyber Rifles, on Easter Monday 1930.

Damaged by a V2 flying bomb in July 1944, the Castle, which had been modernised in 1939, did not re-open until 1946. It closed in 1959, but was not demolished until some years later. This 1965 view shows its terminal decline.

The Art-Deco County Cinema, designed by Edgar Simmons, seated 1158 in comfort. It opened in July 1933 with *Blonde Venus* in which Marlene Dietrich appeared in a gorilla suit. The County closed in October 1982 and was demolished for an office block.

Eight

Military Matters

O. Wigginton (centre) at Volunteer camp in the 1890s; they became the Hertfordshire Regiment in 1908.

Sheehan, Bandmaster of the Hertford Militia, and his band, Light Horse Troop, South Herts Yeomanry, around 1840.

Officers of the Herts Yeomanry Cavalry, mounted drill order, with female visitors, c. 1895.

First Hertfordshire Volunteer Batallion of the Bedfordshire Regiment, full dress walking out order, includes Captain Crawley in the back row, third from right, at camp in 1908.

Tea Time. The Herts Guards make camp at Bury St Edmunds in the uneasy summer of 1914. The elaborate dress uniforms had now disappeared.

The cavalry of the Hertfordshire Yeomanry on parade in Fore Street at the turn of the century.

The Fourth Batallion of the Bedfordshire Regiment (together with the first Herts Volunteer Batallion) served in the Boer War, 1899-1902. In July 1902, their Commanding Officer, Viscount Cranborne, received the Freedom of the Borough at the Corn Exchange.

The 2/1st Herts Regiment musketry team won cups in the 207th Brigade Championship, held in 1916 in the middle of the First World War.

The 2/1st Herts Regiment served in the war of attrition in north-east France until the Armistice of November 11 1918. Colonel John Sainsbury (right) and R. D. Oldham (left) stand in the trenches on the Somme.

Above: The elegant Greek style No. 2 North Road, built in 1827-8 for himself by the architect Thomas Smith, was, by the early twentieth century, the home of Dr Burnett-Smith and his wife, the novelist and social activist, Annie Swan.

Left: On October 13 1915, a Zeppelin flew low over Hertford, and unloaded its bombs. Among the damaged buildings was the servants' wing of No. 2 North Road, but the main house sustained little damage.

Above: Bull Plain bore the brunt of the Zeppelin raid, with Nos 25, 27 and 29 shattered. Four citizens, including the Borough Surveyor, Mr Gregory, were killed when they emerged from Lombard House nearby, to see the airship illuminated by searchlights.

Right: Properties in Hertford Heath, south-east of the town: residents pose in a bomb crater in their garden.

Only practice, but war was in the air in 1938, air-raid shelters had been prepared, and Major R. Whitaker was in charge of ARP services.

The ARP station on Mill Bridge was protected with sandbags in 1940. This was scant protection against the V2 raid on 2 July 1944.

Mill Bridge and the mills took the full force of the blast which wrecked Ilott's and Nicholls' shops, damaged the Woolpack Inn and Castle Cinema, and left a trail of destruction on the banks of the Lea.

A panoramic view from the roof of McMullen's offices in Cowbridge revealed the extent of the damage to the Old Cross frontage.

After the conflict, Queen Elizabeth, as Honorary Colonel of the Hertfordshire Regiment, attended a rally and parade at County Hall on July 21 1946.

Accompanied by the Lord Lieutenant, Viscount Hampden, Her Majesty spoke to veterans of the Boer War, and the two World Wars.

Nine

Moving with the Times

The first traffic lights in Hertford, at the junction of Fore Street and South Street, were switched on by Cllr. G. L. Mansfield, Chairman of the Highways Committee, in August 1936: the era of traffic control had begun.

Up, up and away. On 1-2 July 1891 a grand bazaar to raise money to build St Nicholas Hall was held on Christ's Hospital cricket field. A highlight was the first balloon ascent in Hertford, photographed by Elsden.

The Eastern Counties Railway reached Hertford in October 1843. Taken into the Great Eastern system, the railhead was moved to Mill Road and an imposing Jacobean-style terminus was constructed in 1888. The Station Hotel (now The Dolphin) can be seen in the background.

A quiet platform scene shows the cast-iron columns and braces supporting the platform canopies. In the distance the buffer lights, brought from the earlier station in Railway Place can be glimpsed.

The rival Great Northern Railway reached Cowbridge in 1858 with a branch from Welwyn. Its station building was plain and utilitarian with a rash of advertisements.

The Great Northern line ran across Hartham to connect with the GER. The track bed is now a car park, and the site of the station, which closed in 1924, has been absorbed into McMullen's Brewery.

This view shows the junction of North Road and Sandy Hill just before construction of the new bridge to take the GNR to Watton-at-Stone, and Hertford North station. Shortly after completion, the line was absorbed into the LNER system. The distant rail bridge, now demolished except for one abutment, carried the Cowbridge line to Welwyn.

Construction of the new Great Northern line from Enfield to Stevenage immediately followed the First World War. The embankment at Horns Mill Road is seen under construction. The line opened in 1920.

Old and new. One of Wren's horse-drawn vans and a motor bus seen in Fore Street, in 1925, outside The Chequer Inn, by then an insurance office and soon to be demolished.

Opposite above: Slum clearance of the congested courts and yards behind the main street, which characterised what a social observer called 'hideous Hertford' began in the nineteenth century. These houses in Railway Street, near Old Workhouse Yard, were demolished in 1888 for Market Street.

Opposite below: A legacy of unfit housing lasted well into the present century. In 1932, these houses stood at the foot of Peg's Lane near the junction with Castle Street. In the distance is the newly built Richard Hale School.

Hertford Borough began to construct council housing under the 1919 Housing Act to provide Lloyd George's 'Homes for Heroes'. Hillside Terrace and Pearson Avenue were built in the early 1920s, off Hornsmill and Brickendon Road.

Above: After the Second World War, the Sele Farm Estate reflected the progressive architecture of the nearby new towns at Hatfield and Welwyn.

Opposite above: In 1935 an architectural competition for the new County Hall, on the Leahoe estate in Peg's Lane, was won by James and Bywaters with Rowland Pierce. Miskin & Sons of St Albans were the main contractors and this 1938 photograph shows construction well under way.

Opposite below: The building was completed in the summer of 1939, and the County Council met in the new Council Chamber shortly before the Second World War erupted on 3 September.

The seventeenth-century Old Coffee House in Maidenhead Street was demolished in 1938 for the new Burton's tailors, but a few carved studs were preserved in Hertford Museum.

After the war many Hertford buildings looked shabby. The Enfield Highway Co-operative Society hoped to redevelop Dimsdale House in Bull Plain. Eventually this fine Queen Anne house was saved and restored to win an Architectural Heritage Year Award in 1975.

The crowded courts of Bircherley Green were partly cleared in the interwar years to form an open market, but left ugly gaps in the Railway Street frontage. In the background is the cowl of Priory Street Maltings, now converted into old people's accommodation.

The car park and bus station looked bleak and windswept in February 1944. In the distance is the old Hertford Ragged School. Bircherley Green was redeveloped in the 1980s for a modern shopping precinct and multi-storey car park.

Not a bomb site but road works for Gascoyne Way at the roundabout junction with
Hertingfordbury Road and Cross Lane. In the background of this May 1964 photograph is
St Andrew's church.

Opposite above: Under construction in 1979, a concrete and steel viaduct strides across the meads
and leaps over the Ware Road in the background, by-passing the town centre of Ware on the
busy A10 trunk route.

Opposite below: A train crosses the flooded King's Meads in this late nineteenth century Elsden
photograph – what a contrast to today!

NEAR THIS SPOT WAS HELD
THE FIRST GENERAL SYNOD
OF THE ENGLISH CHURCH
ON 24. SEPTEMBER 673. A.D.
UNDER THE PRESIDENCY OF
THEODORE OF TARSUS
SEVENTH ARCHBISHOP OF
CANTERBURY AND FIRST
PRIMATE OF ALL ENGLAND.

THERE WERE PRESENT
BISI · BISHOP OF EAST ANGLIA
PUTTA · BISHOP OF ROCHESTER
ELEUTHERIUS · BISHOP OF WESSEX
WINFRED · BISHOP OF MERCIA
AND
WILFRED · BISHOP OF NORTHUMBRIA

Above: The 1300th anniversary of the First General Synod of the English Church at Hertford was commemorated in September 1973. Robert Runcie, then Bishop of St Albans, chats to Archbishop Heenan of Westminster.

Left: A commemorative stone had been placed in the Castle grounds in 1935.

Opposite: The former chapel at Christ's Hospital was demolished in 1987, following the closure of the school, and its site is now part of the Tesco supermarket car park.

Castle Hall, with its striking maltings roof, was built in 1976-9 and designed by Shingler Risdon Associates to occupy the site fronting The Wash, formerly occupied by the Castle Cinema and part of the Town Mill.

Above: Town-twinning. Mayors S. W. Andrews (Hertford) and Henri Brun (Evron) preside over a ceremony linking their historical towns in friendship, held on 9 May 1977.

Right: Cyril Heath, journalist on the Hertfordshire Mercury, and local historian, presents HM The Queen Mother with a copy of *The Book of Hertford* at the County Show, in 1974.

Left: Restored in 1989-90 to commemorate the centenary of Hertfordshire County Council, the Adam Assembly Room provided a model for a scene in Jane Austen's *Pride and Prejudice*, where Elizabeth Bennet first met Mr Darcy at a brilliant ball.

Below: The restored Shire Hall, with its reinstated 'Grand Window', forms a backdrop to 'Confluence', a sculpture by William Pye, a gift to the town under a legacy from Mrs Elsie Medlock, and the brain child of Alan Melville, founder Chairman and President of Hertford Civic Society. 'Confluence', located in Salisbury Square, was dedicated on 11 December 1994.